First World War
and Army of Occupation
War Diary
France, Belgium and Germany

57 DIVISION
171 Infantry Brigade
King's (Liverpool Regiment)
2/8 Battalion
1 September 1915 - 1 February 1916

WO95/2983/6

The Naval & Military Press Ltd
www.nmarchive.com
Published in association with The National Archives

Published by

The Naval & Military Press Ltd

Unit 10 Ridgewood Industrial Park,

Uckfield, East Sussex,

TN22 5QE England

Tel: +44 (0) 1825 749494

www.naval-military-press.com

www.nmarchive.com

This diary has been reprinted in facsimile from the original. Any imperfections are inevitably reproduced and the quality may fall short of modern type and cartographic standards.

© Crown Copyright
Images reproduced by permission of The National Archives, London, England, 2015.

Contents

Document type	Place/Title	Date From	Date To
Heading	WO95/2983/6 57 Div 171 Infantry Bde 2/8 Btn Kings Liverpool Regt Aug 1915-Feb 1916		
Heading	Summary Of 2nd Line 8th (Irish) Bn. "The King's Liverpool Regiment For August 1915		
Miscellaneous	Summary	03/09/1915	03/09/1915
Heading	War Diary Of 2nd Line 8th (Irish) Bn. "The King's" Liverpool Regiment For September 1915		
War Diary	Canterbury	01/09/1915	30/09/1915
Heading	War Diary Of 2nd Line 8th (Irish) Bn. "The King's" Liverpool Regiment For October 1915		
War Diary	Canterbury	01/10/1915	31/10/1915
Heading	War Diary Of 2nd Line 8th (Irish) Bn. "The King's Liverpool Regiment November 1915		
War Diary	Canterbury	01/11/1915	30/11/1915
Heading	War Diary Of 2nd Line 8th (Irish) Bn. "The King's" Liverpool Regiment December 1915		
War Diary	Canterbury	01/12/1915	31/12/1915
Heading	War Diary Of 2nd Line 8th (Irish) Bn. "The King's Liverpool Regiment January 1916		
War Diary	Canterbury	01/01/1916	31/01/1916
Heading	War Diary Of 2nd Line 8th (Irish) Bn. "The King's Liverpool Regiment February 1916		
War Diary	Canterbury	01/02/1916	29/01/1916

WO95/2983/6

57 DIV

171 INFANTRY BDE

2/6 BTN KINGS LIVERPOOL REGT

Aug 1915 - Oct 1916

171 BDE

Confidential

Summary

of

2nd LINE 8th (IRISH) Bn. "THE KING'S" LIVERPOOL REGIMENT.

for August 1915

[signature] CAPT. & ADJT.
2nd LINE 8th (IRISH) Bn. "THE KING'S" LIVERPOOL REGIMENT.

SUMMARY.

UNIT. 2nd Line 8th (Irish) Bn. "The King's" (L'pool Regt.).

BRIGADE. 171st Infantry Brigade.

DIVISION. 57th (West Lancashire) Division.

MOBILIZATION CENTRE. Liverpool.

TEMPORARY WAR STATION. Canterbury.

STATIONS OCCUPIED SUBSEQUENT TO CONCENTRATION.   Blackpool.

(a) Mobilization. — Battalion formed 2.12.1914 at Blackpool. Recruits obtained from Liverpool, Preston, Blackpool, Lancaster and Fleetwood.

(b) Concentration at War Station including Railway move. — Move from Blackpool to Canterbury 19.4.1915.

(c) Organization for Defence (including vulnerable points). — Nil.

(d) Training. — All elementary training satisfactorily carried out. 782 completed General Musketry Course. (This is in addition to 186 other ranks already sent to 1st Line Unit Overseas). Field Training carried out.

(e) Discipline. Good.

(f) Administration:-
   (1) Medical Service.   Good.
   (2) Vet'y Services.   Good.
   (3) Supply.   Good.
   (4) Transport.   Good.
   (5) Ordnance.   Good.
   (6) Billetting and Hutting.   Excellent.
   (7) Channels of Correspondence. 171st Infantry Brigade.
   (8) Range Construction.   Nil.
   (9) Remounts.   Good.

(g) Reorganization into Home and Imperial Service. — Has been carried out.

(h) Preparation for Imperial Service. — The whole of the Battalion is for Imperial Service. 15 Officers and 186 other ranks have been sent as reinforcements to 1st Line Unit with Expeditionary Force in France

Old Park, Canterbury.
3rd September 1915.

War Diary

of

2nd LINE 8th (IRISH) Bn. "THE KING'S" LIVERPOOL REGIMENT.

for

September 1915.

Army Form C. 2118.

WAR DIARY
or
INTELLIGENCE SUMMARY.
(*Erase heading not required.*)

Instructions regarding War Diaries and Intelligence Summaries are contained in F. S. Regs., Part II. and the Staff Manual respectively. Title pages will be prepared in manuscript.

Hour, Date, Place	Summary of Events and Information	Remarks and references to Appendices
CANTERBURY. 1.9.1915.	Bayonet Fighting by night commenced.	
2.9.1915.	Lieut-Col. J.A. Cooney gazetted to Territorial Force Reserve. Field Operations.	
3.9.1915.	Nil.	
4.9.1915.	Route March.	
5.9.1915.	Nil	
6.9.1915.	Night Operations.	
7.9.1915.	Nil.	
8.9.1915.	Battalion moves from Hutments, Old Park, into billets in Canterbury City.	
9.9.1915.	Nil.	
10.9.1915.	Nil.	
11.9.1915.	Route March.	
12.9.1915.	Nil.	
13.9.1915.	Night Operations.	
14.9.1915.	Nil.	
15.9.1915.	Night Operations.	
16.9.1915.	Field Operations.	
17.9.1915.	Nil.	
18.9.1915.	2/Lieut. J.N.L. Bryan reports for duty from 3rd Line Depot. Route March.	
19.9.1915.	Nil.	
20.9.1915.	Night Operations.	
21.9.1915.	Nil.	
22.9.1915.	Night Operations.	
23.9.1915.	Field Operations.	
24.9.1915.	Nil.	
25.9.1915	Route March.	
26.9.1915.	Nil.	
27.9.1915.	Night Operations.	
28.9.1915.	Nil.	
29.9.1915.	Night Operations.	
30.9.1915.	Field Operations. 2/Lieut. H. Wilson reports for duty from 3rd Line Depot.	

Confidential

War Diary

of

2nd LINE 8th (IRISH) Bn. "THE KING'S" LIVERPOOL REGIMENT.

for October 1915.

2nd LINE 8th (IRISH) Bn. "THE KING'S" LIVERPOOL REGIMENT.

Army Form C. 2118

WAR DIARY
or
INTELLIGENCE SUMMARY
(Erase heading not required.)

Instructions regarding War Diaries and Intelligence Summaries are contained in F.S. Regs., Part II. and the Staff Manual respectively. Title Pages will be prepared in manuscript.

Place	Date	Hour	Summary of Events and Information	Remarks and references to Appendices
Canterbury.	Oct. 1915.			
	1.		Lieut-Colonel G. Rippon assumes command. Field Operations.	
	2.		Nil.	
	3.		Nil.	
	4.		Nil.	
	5.		Route March.	
	6.		Nil.	
	7.		Battalion moves out of billets to the Hutments, Old Park, Canterbury.	
	8.		Night Operations.	
	9.		Officer Commanding 57th W.L.D. Train Inspects Transport.	
	10.		Nil.	
	11.		Nil.	
	12.		Nil.	
	13.		Battalion parade for selection of Munition Workers.	
	14.		Nil.	
	15.		Fire Alarm Practice. Night Operations.	
	16.		Nil.	
	17.		Nil.	
	18.		Battalion Kit Inspection.	
	19.		Nil.	
	20.		Nil.	
	21.		Nil.	
	22.		Night Operations.	
	23.		Nil.	
	24.		Nil.	
	25.		Nil.	
	26.		Nil.	
	27.		Nil.	
	28.		Nil.	
	29.		Alarm Practices at 12 noon and 5.30 p.m.	
	30.		Route March.	
	31.		Nil.	

Confidential

171 BDE

War Diary

of

2nd LINE 8th (IRISH) Bn. "THE KING'S" LIVERPOOL REGIMENT.

November 1915.

Army Form C. 2118

WAR DIARY
INTELLIGENCE SUMMARY
(Erase heading not required.)

Instructions regarding War Diaries and Intelligence Summaries are contained in F.S. Regs., Part II. and the Staff Manual respectively. Title Pages will be prepared in manuscript.

Place	Date	Hour	Summary of Events and Information	Remarks and references to Appendices
Canterbury.	Nvr. 1.		Nil.	
	2.		Nil.	
	3.		Nil.	
	4.		Nil.	
	5.		Nil.	
	6.		Nil.	
	7.		Informed by 171st Brigade that a Zeppelin Raid may be expected at an early date.	
	8.		Nil.	
	9.		Nil.	
	10.		Nil.	
	11.		"D" Company placed in Quarantine owing to suspected outbreak of diphtheria.	
	12.		Nil.	
	13.		Nil.	
	14.		Nil.	
	15.		Nil.	
	16.		"D" Company released from Quarantine.	
	17.		Nil.	
	18.		Nil.	
	19.		Nil.	
	20.		Nil.	
	21.		Nil.	
	22.		The Bn. was inspected by Brigadier-General A.R.Gilbert, D.S.O.	
	23.		Alarm Practice, 5 p.m.	
	24.		Nil.	
	25.		The Bn. was inspected by Major General E.T.Dickson, Inspector of Infantry.	
	26.		Alarm Practice, 4 p.m.	
	27.		Nil.	
	28.		Fire Alarm Practice, 8-30 p.m. Fire broke out in Officers' Qtrs. Extinguished after 10 minutes.	
	29.		Court of Enquiry assembled re fire.	
	30.		Alarm Practice, 5 p.m.	

E. Pipper.
LIEUT. COLONEL
COMMANDING 2nd LINE 8th (IRISH) Bn. "THE KING'S" LIVERPOOL REGT.

Confidential

War Diary

of

2nd LINE 8th (IRISH) Bn. "THE KING'S" LIVERPOOL REGIMENT.

December 1915.

Army Form C. 2118

WAR DIARY
INTELLIGENCE SUMMARY
(Erase heading not required.)

Instructions regarding War Diaries and Intelligence Summaries are contained in F.S. Regs., Part II. and the Staff Manual respectively. Title Pages will be prepared in manuscript.

Place	Date Dec. 15.	Hour	Summary of Events and Information	Remarks and references to Appendices
Canterbury.	1	—	Nil.	
	2	—	Nil.	
	3	—	Nil.	
	4	—	Nil.	
	5	—	Nil.	
	6	—	Nil.	
	7	—	Nil.	
	8	—	Nil.	
	9	—	Nil.	
	10	—	Nil.	
	11	—	Nil.	
	12	—	Nil.	
	13	—	Night Operations. Nil.	
	14	—	Nil.	
	15	—	Nil.	
	16	—	Nil.	
	17	—	Nil.	
	18	—	Nil.	
	19	—	Nil.	
	20	—	Nil.	
	21	—	Alarm Practice, 2-30 p.m.	
	22	—	Nil.	
	23	—	Nil.	
	24	—	Nil.	
	25	—	Nil.	
	26	—	Nil.	
	27	—	Nil.	
	28	—	Nil.	
	29	—	Nil.	
	30	—	Alarm Practice, 8 p.m.	
	31	—	Nil.	

E. Rippon.
LIEUT. COLONEL,
COMMANDING 2nd LINE 8th (IRISH) Bn. "THE KING'S" L'POOL REGT.

Canterbury. 3-1-1916

Confidential

War Diary
of

2nd LINE 8th (IRISH) Bn. "THE KING'S" LIVERPOOL REGIMENT.

January 1916

Army Form C. 2118

WAR DIARY
INTELLIGENCE SUMMARY
(Erase heading not required.)

Instructions regarding War Diaries and Intelligence Summaries are contained in F. S. Regs., Part II. and the Staff Manual respectively. Title Pages will be prepared in manuscript.

Place	Date Jan. 1916.	Hour	Summary of Events and Information	Remarks and references to Appendices
Canterbury	1	-	Nil.	f.
	2	-	Nil.	f.
	3	-	Nil.	f.
	4	12-30 p.m.	Inspection by Lieut-General Sir C.L.Woollcombe K.C.B. Commanding II Army.	f.
	5	-	Nil.	f.
	6	-	Nil.	f.
	7	-	Nil.	f.
	8	-	Nil.	f.
	9	-	Nil.	f.
	10	-	Nil.	f.
	11	-	Nil.	f.
	12	-	Nil.	f.
	13	-	Nil.	f.
	14	-	Nil.	f.
	15	-	Nil.	f.
	16	-	Nil.	f.
	17	-	Nil.	f.
	18	-	Nil.	f.
	19	-	Nil.	f.
	20	-	Nil.	f.
	21	-	Nil.	f.
	22	-	Nil.	f.
	23	-	Nil.	f.
	24	3-0 p.m.	Fire Alarm.	f.
	25	-	Nil.	f.
	26	-	Nil.	f.
	27	-	Nil.	f.
	28	7-0 p.m.	Alarm Practice.	f.
	29	-	Nil.	f.
	30	-	Nil.	f.
	31	4-0 p.m.	Alarm Practice.	f.

E. Ruxx.

LIEUT. COLONEL,
COMMANDING 2nd LINE 8th (IRISH) Bn. "THE KING'S" L'POOL REGT.

Confidential

War Diary

of

2nd LINE 8th (IRISH) Bn. "THE KING'S" LIVERPOOL REGIMENT.

February 1916.

Army Form C. 2118

WAR DIARY
~~INTELLIGENCE SUMMARY~~
(Erase heading not required.)

Instructions regarding War Diaries and Intelligence Summaries are contained in F. S. Regs., Part II. and the Staff Manual respectively. Title Pages will be prepared in manuscript.

Place	Date 1916	Hour	Summary of Events and Information	Remarks and references to Appendices
Canterbury.	Feby. 1.	–	Nil.	So.
	2.	–	Nil.	So.
	3.	–	Nil.	So.
	4.	–	Nil.	So.
	5.	–	Nil.	So.
	6.	–	Nil.	So.
	7.	–	Nil.	So.
	8.	–	Nil.	So.
	9.	–	Nil.	So.
	10.	–	Nil.	So.
	11.	–	Nil.	So.
	12.	–	Nil.	So.
	13.	–	Nil.	So.
	14.	–	Nil.	So.
	15.	–	Nil.	So.
	16.	5-30 p.m.	Alarm.	So.
	17.	–	Nil.	So.
	18.	–	Nil.	So.
	19.	–	Nil.	So.
	20.	–	Nil.	So.
	21.	4 p.m.	Fire Alarm.	So.
	22.	–	Nil.	So.
	23.	–	Nil.	So.
	24.	11-15 a.m.	Telephone Message from Bde. to hold Bn. in readiness to move. First line transport immediately loaded and all preparations made.	So.
	25.	–	Battalion held in readiness to move at an hour's notice.	So.
	26.	–	Battalion held in readiness to move at an hour's notice.	So.
	27.	–	Battalion held in readiness to move at an hour's notice.	So.
	28.	–	Battalion held in readiness to move at an hour's notice.	So.
	29.	6 p.m.	Alarm practice. Bn. held in readiness to move at an hour's notice.	So.

E.J. Parker.

LIEUT. COLONEL,
COMMANDING 2nd LINE 8th (IRISH) Bn. "THE KING'S" L'POOL REGT.

www.ingramcontent.com/pod-product-compliance
Lightning Source LLC
Chambersburg PA
CBHW081511160426
43193CB00014B/2656